AMOR

THE STORY OF A LOVE IN 227 POEMS

POETRY BY
INA SCHRODERS-ZEEDERS

Winter Goose
Publishing

Winter Goose Publishing
2701 Del Paso Road, 130-92
Sacramento, CA 95835

www.wintergoosepublishing.com
Contact Information: info@wintergoosepublishing.com

Amor

COPYRIGHT © 2013 by Ina Schroders-Zeeders

ISBN: 978-0-9894792-6-4

First Edition, September 2013

Cover Art by Winter Goose Publishing
Typeset by Odyssey Books

Published in the United States of America

For my sons: Arjen, Tossing, and Maarten
and my granddaughter Eline

Contents

Prologue to Love

1 Suspended Phase

My gait is now not touching ground,
a moment long I'm more than genes insist,
between the gravity and reason I am free,
suspended is my phase, the summit of my run.
What birds can take for granted, now is mine,
a fraction of a second's twist,
not much, almost enough to fly.

It's in these particles of time
I see the truth of what may lie ahead
but after landing, all has left the mind;
the phase is over where feet meet soil.
No more am I a bird, detached from earth.
My body, now a chunk of lead,
feels as I'm just about to die.

Forgotten thoughts are leaving fast
and newer ones emerge by every move.
A run is feast for what's oblivious:
between the body and the soul seems air.
I needed time to contemplate this life
in fractions of my body, prove
to myself: almost enough am I.

Part 1
The Beginning of Love

Poems 2-54

2 Please Find Me

Maybe it's worse to be unfound,
I stick to what I know is true.
Both my feet are on the ground,
I can not run from what is me.
But I am me, is it enough,
there is no secret in my soul,
to find safety, to find love.
I knew you once, loved you before.
I am this, more or less, I'm whole,
so find me please in time once more,
or leave me be just as I am.
I am alone now, bare and cold.

3 Meeting

There might be an announcement when we meet,
a sign perhaps so that we are aware
we should be standing still and talk a bit:
the start of pouring rain, a sunlight beam,
a tribal dance of fireflies above,
to make us see the moment's splendour. May
the gods be bothered, only a little.
Humans on the road of life, encounter
of two more souls finding a mate by chance.
I do not know this as you walk my way.

4 Jugendstil

We stood, one in sculpture,
our curves stretched and shining
in moonlight. It was summer
and we were near the river Rhine.

Nothing to say as we were statues,
we watched the world die
in meteor rain and thunder storm.

Around us destruction,
we didn't move,
we now were lovers, one
in the last moments of our sculptured youth.

5 Awaiting the Ferry with You on Board

Awaiting the ferry, how it would be
to be now with you and how you would see
the island come closer and nearer.

To you it must be as if moving is me,
that I am the one crossing the sea
to be in a place so much dearer.

6 It's There

Detect my hidden love for you,
look for it, dare to find,
it is not hidden all that well,
just peek over my fence,
kill all the dragons,
call me by my name.

Open me. Just crack my shell.
Skin maybe between our flesh,
words come between our thinking.
I cry through layers of grief
and my sound is smothered by
what culture asks of me.

Find me through layers,
dig deeper and search well
in mazes, and in mist
and everywhere,
and like you do,
I shall. I shall,
and find, as it is there.

7 Knowing

Across a crowded room
where some were celebrating
but we only came to be out of the rain,
I tried to ignore your eyes.
I thought I didn't know your eyes then
yet they knew me,
and they were smiling at me
so I looked back.

I must have remembered you
from another life
or from a glimpse into the future.
We stepped out into the rain together.
No one missed us at the party.

8 You Hit My Nerve

Under all the layers of indifference
there was a hidden nerve embedded well,
escaping balance of my bivalence,
so what was true or not, I could not tell.

There had been days that would have made some sense,
but most of them were like small stones that fell
out of the past into the present tense.
They left so fast, I had no time to dwell.

Yet underneath all was a slumbering
that only had to be revealed by love
Dealt with items on my numbering
I realized that you were so enough.

With patience no one had, your caring
life got much better, I emerged the rough.
The layers have cracked, there was an opening,
all of a sudden I was not that tough.
Your presence and much more your lingering
meant my indifference had to back off.

9 In Another Life I Knew You

You stood there under bricks that formed a bow,
I saw you there, before you came my way,
before you were my life, already so
you were a part of me, and you will stay.

We haven't lived before, I can't believe
some hundred years ago we, too, were here,
us being lovers then; that's so naïve,
a love through time that would not disappear?

But still you know me and I know you, too,
and when you talk, it's like I've always known
the words you say, the moves, the things you do
as an eternity to call our own.

You stood there under bricks that formed a bow,
before you were my life, already so.

10 You Don't Know Me

I saved your words out of the spam
and in my bed I read them loud,
your words are what my life's about,
how well you know me in your verse
but you don't know me.

The snow keeps falling over buds
while flowers should be screaming out,
their lives seem lost in silenced doubt
that there will be a spring again
as they don't know that.

I keep the poem and the buds,
and shiver now I do without
your smile. You touched a dying sprout.
How well you know me in your verse.
But you don't know me.

11 Pretend We Are Together

We have been taught to read with caution
as letters need to mean the same each time they show.
But the creative child that makes up a new meaning
sees more in each word than a word as is.

He finds the magic of the mind that lets the logic go.
I read in your eyes more than they do tell me,
and I know it, and still I am content.
Let's be creative and wonder through those landscapes
never to be ours, but always in our thoughts,
forbidden places where we never went.

We walk a nonexisting road and sleep in beds together
where we have never slept, feel the linen touch our skin.
Smell the sea and tar from at the harbours.
We can pretend we share a moment in a different town,
we can pretend we are creative, and that I have let you in.

12 How to Know

If someone told me
it's me you're in love with
I would think him
a liar maybe.

If someone was sure
you had noticed me
I would not believe him
for a moment.

Nobody ever
told me such a thing
so just how am I to know
anyway

that it could be real
what he did not say?
If only someone
had told me this.

I go by his unspoken words
and hope
that you have noticed me
in fact,

how else
to keep the dream intact
that you will be my love
one day?

13 To Be So In Love

To be so in love
that you forget to eat,
that you can only think of your loved one's eyes,
that cold rain feels pleasant to you,
that you don't need sleep yet always dream,
that you write poems in spite of dyslexia,
and watching the full moon makes you smile,
okay we all can do that, but

to be so in love
that trees start to shiver when you pass them by,
that birds on their way south fly back to greet you,
that mountains roll over to let you go through,
and the moon has decided to shine full and round
though it is that time of month when it is new,
now that is
to be so in love.

14 Undressed for the Occasion

Like an unnecessary metaphor
not adding anything,
the evening comes
uninvited and too early
in a long, black dress,
tight, with too much glitter,
and she doesn't have the sense to slip
into something more comfy.

What can we say when we know
the night is approaching with the hour,
and we can't stay together?
We look at her and we hate her.
There is so much we want to tell
each other. But she had to show up.
Ignoring her won't help.
She yawns and grins a lot, her breath is sour.

See how she is trying to sit it out
with a tear in the back of the dress, haha,
while in any other garment
she might have had a ball.
Evenings should only wear
comfort jeans or sexy baby dolls perhaps,
or leave us be together;
we who fear the black dressed night.

15 Best to Ignore

Like dealing with an illness, it is best
to ignore my feelings, give it rest,
for more, I know, will never be our truth,
it is a memory from then, our youth
when we were lovers, strangers on our quest
starting with our lives, fleeing from the nest.
For more, I know, will never be our truth,
it is a memory from then, our youth.

16 A Tree

This tree just started life
and will be here perhaps
when mine is over,
and it will know the warmth of summers
that I shall never see,
feel the frost in every vein in winters.
Why care for this tree?

This tree will be here
when we have long perished
and its leaves will blow over our graves.
By then, have we known love at all,
not just words, a silly feel of danger?
Or were our lives wasted?
Why care for a stranger?

It doesn't matter to the tree
if it knew me or not
and I, too, must let go
of thoughts and this earth,
go on to where it sleeps,
accept you were merely polite
when you kissed my lips.

17 Clouds

As the clouds grow bigger over my head
I sit down, watch how the spectacle floats,
the shades changing from snow to those of lead,
watch faces transform into jumping goats.

I write on white spots in fading bright blue
that are taken by the wind over sea,
watch them grow, to grey and black towards you
where my words will be raining, endlessly.

18 Shaped

layer by layer you took whom I was
with every piece of clothing, with every word
you whispered, something new came out of me.

you went through my skin, you went in me, found
what I hide, you took it and replaced it
layer by layer, you made me be yours.

19 Dealing While Dreaming

You look at me with questions so intense
of matters known, those not to be put lightly
in logic places. Do not try reason.
Feelings, ghosts without a mating season
of their own, let's deal with them in nightly
hours, dreaming, while our minds never make sense.

20 You Left Your Coat

You stood on my doorstep one night
asking for shelter in another language,
but the weather was fine.

I found some wine while you got out of your wet coat
and all your other clothes that were soaked as well.
But the weather was dry. The water was salt.

Layer by layer, wool from the Shetland islands,
a linen shirt that was made in Italy,
and a scarf you claimed a woman in Greece had knitted.
I could sense her scent, spicy and sweet.

I took you into my bed and warmed you
for days with my body.
You never told me the name of your ship
but left your coat when you went.
It never dried up all together.

21 After All

In the end,
after all of the drama,
the night did now silence,
the town tried to sleep
and we were together.

We, the battered,
in this salty morning mist,
you and me, facing the cliff,
where I reached for your hand,
afraid I would fall.

I wanted to live.
You took it.
We had nothing to say.
What else could have mattered.

The sun came and shone
on our skin and our hair
through every layer
of yesterday's grey.

22 The End of the Best of Dreams

I'm embraced in warmest welcome then
(this is my favourite part of the dream)
I come home, anywhere, and feel safe.
You are there, and we cry, for all that was,
we made it, both, with everyone we love.
I shall continue to dream every night
till I wake up in the truth of this dream.

23 Say Nothing More

when nothing matters more than arms around you,
say nothing more and let your body do the talking
I want to feel as much as possible of your embrace
words will come later
now nothing matters more than arms around us
say nothing more

24 Mind is Path

Beginning their way, thoughts are as sound bites,
flickering neon signs, fragments of words
the memory of scent that lingered in a lover's hair.

Like scattered reflections
of a world that's on the move
they assemble into reason,
with each step providing proof
that mind is path to finding truth.
It was the feather I found
that reminded me of your hair
and all that came with a day on the beach.
My thoughts have found a true path, each.

25 No Rings Needed

Come one evening to my house,
and we'll watch the sun go down,
while the bird that has no name
sings to us till it is dawn.

Come this evening, as my spouse,
hear the church bells across town;
none will ever be the same,
out-of-wedlock we'll go on.

26 Affected

I'm affected by you much,
still, why can't I feel there's sense—
is there purpose, is there use
to a love without a touch,
to a gate without a fence?
I'm affected much and loose.

27 The Words Repeat Ourselves

So many words come
silently in repeat,
they're those for you
to find and read.

Words, like birds,
black white feathers spread,
that don't make sense
until you dream your sleep.

So dream and think
of words you read to me,
so many words, all meant to be,
may come in repeat.

Silently you'll find them deep,
and somewhere in between
find me, find me, do,
as I come along with them.

So many words
come in repeat, you see.
They all say: yes, I do love you.
Now make that words that show.

28 Cliché

They didn't last;
like hallucinations
in a feverish episode
popping up unexpectedly
with brightness, though
in night's darkest hour—
they faded before
the surprise was gone.

When these words sank in,
the moment was over.
I love you, he said.
And he had meant it.

29 Timeless Moment

I do not know the name of day today
and what hour it is I do not care,
my thoughts are cluttered much
around one moment long ago,
I relive it on and on,
my time has stopped for now,
for then it was forever
between me and you.
We let a dove fly out its cage.
It never did come back.

30 I Need You With Me

Being near you makes me warmer,
my bones, my skin, my heart, my words
all need you to forget the cold
that other people gave me
that I gave to myself,
I need you with me
to forget how much cold hurts.

31 Someone Just Like You

To be alone, in times
that I would rather be with you
or someone just like you perhaps,
and walk a road, almost alone
almost with someone just like you,
to be a dreamer on my road,
perhaps it's time to be just that.

32 Grains of Drifting Sand

All the grains of sand blowing senseless over land
like how my thoughts are moving towards you
away from reason and from solid ground,
they go into directions I don't understand.

33 A House on the Island of Naxos

It was a perfect house, not ours, but of a friend
of yours, whose grandma lived there years ago, and nothing
had been moved nor touched since then. Nobody lived there
and nobody cared we opened the front door with force.
Upstairs we had no time to lose and took off all our clothes
before we found a bed, our bodies needed to be close and closer, more
so as the night was almost gone, and ghosts
took over the dark floors below us, we went on.
Then we came down into the kitchen, there
they lingered, with accusing eyes and pointing fingers,
guilt was written everywhere in blood.
The house started to scream and cupboards slammed,
we waited till more daylight came, and left apart,
I walked the way to town and never saw you back.
And now I hear the house has been on fire, only days
after our sin, and no one knows how come.

34 We Shall Remain

To see beyond what can be learned with eyes,
to find through your eyes every time we meet
is truth, that gives me joy, comes as surprise,
so know that I shall follow when you lead.

To be with you. What else should matter to me,
to catch with your hands all that we have found?
This so much gives me life, so let us be
in love together, and forever bound.

To me this is enough to get us by:
to be, after the bad that we have seen,
together. Now: we only have to try
and make it both, in spite of what's obscene.

If we can just forget about the pain,
that came to our lives, we shall remain.

35 Shade of a Storm

As light is needed to make shade, so do
I need your voice to say what's real here, what is made
of substance, what is air and nothing more. Or lies the truth in
the transparent molecules between us when we see each other?
Air has no shade, no memories, you say.

Yet I recall a certain storm we had before.
Air moving fast. Although it didn't last for long,
the memory won't fade. The air between us seems much thicker now.
So what is real when clouds have moved away,
is it enough for us to open savoured bottles? Will you stay?

36 The Right Harbour

Let's say you were the lighthouse.
My ship sailed, abandoned by the mad captain,
the gear all torn up, the anchor lost.

Yes, and then north of your light
I lingered a fortnight not sure of my future,
while storms were battering shores and my ship.

Poorly, awaiting fair weather
in your guiding beams, I found what I searched for.
I hoped on, while clouds kept moving fast.

Surely, now two weeks have passed,
today will be quiet, the water is calmer,
my ship setting sail, your light seems not needed.

Sailing the ship goes, to the horizon
but I'll remain here, in your sight, if you let me,
as here is my harbour, for my years to come.

37 Fusion

so
was it
you read me
could it be like this then
we all have one great soul perhaps
but we let it live in many different bodies
and sometimes the minds embrace each other
and sometimes the bodies melt together
and sometimes both encounters
happen at the same time
like last night
it was
so

38 After Deed

No more united our bodies fell back
on the bed, already lonely,
and we heard the rain again,
life went on again, life we were
not part of
together.
We saw again,
as there was light,
then day turned into night.
We didn't move nor talk,
remaining strangers
awaiting the cold of the dark,
and each on our own.

39 Entering

I remember well that you came in the room
and how you found me, with your eyes.
Their message, soundless, made me blush as it was rude.
The room was full of others, still it was
as if we were alone, and nude.
I felt your touch upon my skin,
though you were near the window,
and I was near the bar.
I couldn't move away from it, I couldn't leave
as you were in the room with me.
Yet you were still too far.
And then I closed my eyes.
I waited till all others left
the room but you.
I waited till you did indeed
caress my skin, opened my eyes
and let you in.

40 We Had the Same Mood

Your eyes told me you felt it too,
and so we stayed together saying nothing,
near the motorway,
we listened to the traffic noise
pretending that it was the sea. It was the sea
and the tarmac our beach. We had the same mood
then. Sometimes I think that day was best.

41 Why I Want You

The curve your neck makes to your shoulders
moves me, more than making love itself,
it's how you bend your head.
I know that other men
have this curve as well,
I would not want them for it.
The fact you have, is why I want you
to make love to me.
Come on.

42 Change of Life

I see you now not like before,
someone who lived and sinned
and cared and cried and more.
Your body is all you, not only
the outside is beautiful to me
in all its aging truth.
The way you are,
is how I want you.
I never wanted just your youth.

43 Like Changing Clouds

It is not over, but the evening clouds
in sweeter shades of blood
make it bearable to have you not here.

Where you are, is the same light,
maybe you are watching
the same clouds, thinking of me.

Do you see how the face of that king
changes into the map of France now
and back to a face with no name?

There is no chance, how could we be together,
but we are together, even apart.
See how we move on like changing clouds
in denial of our hearts. In sweetest colours.

44 Sometimes I See You

Sometimes I see you in a morning cloud,
a friendly face for just a second,
then floating on in horror scenes
and never staying long to be the same,
making me wish I could be there
along with you, move on in air and light.

At times you pop up in a flower bed,
between the colours I can't name,
you are in rivers when the sun is setting,
across the water in some pink and red,
where I see you drifting on
past memories and sweet forevers.

I suppose it is not me
whom you are searching
in clouds and flowers
in singing birds and leafless trees
or in colours drifting to the sea.
I see you anyway
in all that nature shows me.

45 Till Then

I watch you watch the clouds go by
and geese going the same speed,
I see the longing in your eye.
Will they come back, and will we meet?

46 In a Crowd

Eyes finding each other,
recognize, though older, smile,
blink and close.

And when you are almost gone,
moved on in the crowd,
I look over my shoulder.

So do you.
Eyes, do they wink and close?
No one else notices.

Nobody knows.

47 Strangers

Not necessarily are we strangers;
maybe a smile would alter that right now,
if we could forget about the dangers
and if only we remembered how.

48 Be Found in Time

The further you'll be gone in time from me
the more your face will be around in thought
and shall I look in places, never sought
before, to find you in eternity.

You will be everywhere to me, and more
so, please don't dwell away then from the shore,
as I can't go beyond the beach it seems.

No hope for me remains that we will see
each other in reality or dreams,
if you decide to hide in time from me.

The further you'll be gone from me, the more
the beach will be the place where I find thought
to be with you, in our eternity.

49 Conform the Rules of Love

Over cups of coffee and between flaws of life
you reached for my hand in the café.

We didn't say much, just the needed remarks,
an exchange of dull information.

Then your eyes told me more than a phone call would do;
a lonely, troubled soul travelling.

I would have made love to you there and then.
What kept me from doing so, was conformation.

When emptied the cups, going back to our lives
you forgot it of course, as I should do, too.

But the touch of your hand I shall never forget.
In my next life I'll be non-conformist for you.

50 Navy Blue Pullover

The cold is such that canals freeze
and geese are flying south.

I find your navy blue pullover,
put it on.

The fragrance of you lingers
in the woollen/cotton fabric,
caressing me softly,
comforting my skin.

I feel your presence
in the sleeves
that fall over my hands.

I feel your arms
everywhere around,
your warmth
surrounding me.

51 For the Lover

I felt a moment lasting long,
it was a different way of time
and you were there as well, with me.
For a moment I knew love
when I closed my eyes in trust
I felt you were still near and loved.

There will be moments more like this
and when I open my eyes now
you are not gone, you will be here;
remaining lover of my life.

52 Once You Were in This Book

You were somewhere in the pages
hiding and waiting to be found
while I skipped through the book looking
for answers. I finally saw
where I wouldn't look: between lines,
between moments to breathe and read,
there you were, I could feel you, sensed
all about you, your skin on mine
I felt your yearning for love. You
were somewhere in the pages, I
found your hiding place when I stopped
reading, and started loving you.

53 Night

The words had given in to silence now
and evening crawled in shades across the bed.
It had just been five hours since we met,
and now, should I stay or go, and how.

You stood before the window, had a smoke,
the air becoming mist, I saw you fade,
your face was now another's. Had we made
real love or not? No sound. I wished you spoke.

I closed my eyes and waited for your touch.
You threw away the burning cigarette.
Now all was different from when we first met.
The darkness came and didn't care too much.

Why were we in this cheap hotel, this place,
how come I trusted that you cared for me?
So dark it was, but still I learned to see
through tears that were meandering down my face.

I heard you leave the room and fell asleep,
and when the morning came, the sun shone bright,
the room looked different now, so full of light,
and I still loved you, strong and wild and deep.

I tried to stop my tears, and to forget
how much I felt for you, my foolish heart,
I knew I should go on, make a new start,
I took my clothes, and never made the bed.

And then the door went open wide. Right there
you stood, your arms full of roses, red and sweet.
You gave them and you swept me off my feet,
and from that moment, yes, we were a pair.

54 Shelter

I've found a shelter for sad days
when outside hail and thunder rage
and inside all is such a mess,
I don't need blankets to hide under now.
My shelter is to know that you won't run.
I think I found a friend somehow. My search is done.

Part 2
The Best Times Together

Poems 55-132

55 First Time at Last

At last we were us, in a bed after doing it,
after the talks, the drinks, and the fights,
nights were no longer awkward for doing it,
the past let us be for more than awhile.
We had the red tea and croissants to celebrate,
you made a song that you played with a smile.
At last we had found a first time for doing it,
no more fears stuck with it, love conquered hate.

56 Lovers After Being Friends

Like when you touched my face with both your hands,
like when our bodies felt as one, to dare
and see us lovers, after being friends,
together for the first time as a pair,
that is what made this night a memory.
I won't forget the beauty of the blue
we saw above us, and the moon such ivory.
It was our moment, time for me and you
and making love, it felt as if we should
be close together, for as long as we could.

57 In and Out

By every strike as you enter,
there comes the withdraw, when you leave,
when I think that you might be gone forever.

I doubt oceans and shores
feel this joy and abandonation
both lasting just seconds,
every time a wave comes and goes.

What the fuck, they would think,
this will go on forever, in this pace,
higher ashore and then back,
that's the law of the tide.
But they don't know you.

I want to hold you inside
just in case.

58 What the Verb Meant

We rose that day and nothing was the same.
The light to start with had a different name,
the smell had altered in the bedroom air
as we had done it, there and everywhere.

Since we had done it, there and everywhere,
you called us lovers, both, and that seemed fair.
We rose together, nothing was the same,
we knew the meaning of the verb: we came.

59 Forbidden Love

It is in the shiver of the apple tree leaf,
the tremble of the spider's web,
and miles away from there,
the fallen snow, touching the ground.
It is the sound that's everywhere
growing harder, more, to cover
all your crying of this eve,
because you know
you shouldn't love me.

60 Forbidden Loving

Now you have painted, eaten: digest me.
You brought your seed to life in my body;
we are no strangers colliding by chance,
nor can we be anonymous lovers.
Everywhere we'll have a live connection
now you have painted, eaten bread, and seen.

I shall not try to keep you here unseen
where you are only a lover to me,
since to the world you are my connection
guarding over this house and my body,
let them know, let all know we are lovers,
tell them our love is deserving a chance.

All we both ever needed was a chance
to make the world be ours as we had seen.
Stay longer than usually lovers
are together, embrace me, entice me
so I will be more me than my body
and our craving will be our connection.

While you touch me, I feel this connection
as now we are given our second chance
making love undisturbed by somebody.
With all of nature surrounding and seen,
I surrender to feeling you take me
away into the world of free lovers.

We had to secretly become lovers,
trying so hard to hide the connection
between yourself, love, our hide out, and me,
hoping we would not hurt anybody
as long as our love was not to be seen,
but now we have proven we do need a chance.

You painted, ate bread, and loved my body,
in sea blue veils we were silent lovers.
closing our eyes, so it was better seen
where in our minds lied our true connection
knowing there we would both have a chance
for romance, you, my only love, and me.

61 We Were in Whispering Love

How well it is to be with you
during this storm,
to know that we are
now together,
in a place called
"Whispering Love".

The rented bed is ours
for just one night.

Tomorrow may be different
and yesterday I missed you.
This time will be enough
for now.

Take my hand,
nothing is certain.
Yet we are here
to bravely steal this night.

And outside, rain
is battering the windows
over and over again,
gusting wild, moving sand and more
from one place to another.

But we are only us, in such
familiar way together,
in a bed, a room
we never saw before.

We dwell in motions
under black and waving veils
of a ghastly weather.

We hear the storm
while you touch me
and we let Whispering Love,
room number seven,
be our home tonight.

How right it feels
to be with you. To make
love in our rented heaven.

62 Syzygy

I'll take you to the room
where transparent curtains move
and hundreds of candles burn
under a sloping roof.

My whisperings won't turn
into a promise without proof.
The burning shadows learn
to follow how we dance.
I'll teach you how to earn
each moment of romance
in every move, never enough.
Animated, till you find a chance.

You turn me over. Switching
roles and all goes on, a harmony
of you and me, no window do we need above
for astronomic views.

We need no earth, no moon or sun
not even in conjunction,
as we, just two of us, make love.
It is enough.

63 Our First Morning After

We could not rise after this night and go to work.
This was all new, surprised we were,
more so we knew that we had been the first
to find true love and the making of it.

We had discovered heights unknown
to mankind yet, coming before us, after us,
by sharing one old bed. Yes, we were gods.
Thirst drove us down from Olympus.

But the beer was stale. The bread was, too.
You took a fag to deep inhale.
My glasses on, I now could see the time,
and you just saw me different.

The magic went, it drowned itself
in cracked hot mugs of bitter coffee

64 Cupid

Love with all its golden curls had no idea of loving.
I knew that, waking up, covered with torn illusions,
while Cupid stood there, smoking a cigarette,
his pale buttocks more real than the moon as a whole.
Once he loved me, a god he had been in my past.

It was my imperfect body wanting his, but I would have
settled for this double moon and cigarette ashes.
We noticed, though, how love with all its golden curls
left the room through the open window in fumes,
and he put on some clothes.
He was human at last.

65 The Room

You said goodbye when light was not yet here
inside this room, the shelter from our life
where we were make-believe husband and wife.
The artefacts and thoughts were centred clear;
we were ourselves, not mentored, without fear,
no moral guilt to cut us like a knife.
My watch was showing it was half past five
before I dreamt a memory so dear.

When I awoke, the room looked cold and white
as if my clothes had been in brutal fight.
It was how we had left them near the bed
where we pretended we were really wed.
This gave a feeling of a thing not right.
The message that the room silently said
made me not wait for your return that night.

66 The Bed Has No Knowledge

The bed has no knowledge
but there it lies, our love,
in the curves of the sheets
it is hiding, waiting
for our return, now our bodies
are needed elsewhere till dusk.
The bed doesn't know
that it's love. But it's there.

67 Thin Walls of Inappropriate Shame

It made me so proud
walking next to you
the morning after our first time sex
and everyone who saw us,
knew, so I thought.
It was in our eyes
and how we held hands,
but I never was loud,
never shouted your name.
Imagine what memories
we could have made,
if only I had ignored
those thin walls
and my inappropriate shame.

68 Our Walk

We often went there just for silence
to those dunes where you would share
an orange with a seagull.
The colour seemed so out of place,
amidst the grey and beige of winter,
and then go back to warmth of home and good,
our little universe, it seemed it was enough
to build our castle on tranquillity
and sea shells we had taken with us
and like a seagull who loves fruit,
I learned from you to hold and touch
to be content with what we had.
To find the colours in my life.
It was so good, it was our trust.

69 Evenings with You

Our minds have thought alike in our growth
but soul mates is a word we never use
as if to label it would mean to lose
what now is silently between us both.

The evenings seem more bearable somehow
when shared in company of you and wine
and let the storm outside rage on, it's fine;
we have the warmth we need between us now.

To have those nights when your arms shelter me,
it gives me courage to go on with life,
maybe it was wise to become your wife;
I never knew though what you saw in me.

70 Royal Blue Sea

This royal blue sea
on an eve to remember,
imagination.

We have swum together
when darkness set in
and the shore stayed behind.

This royal blue sea
in our imagination;
the colour it was.

71 What Will Stay

What will stay with me most when you are gone:
a whisper on a winter's day in snow,
your eyes when you make love to me perhaps,
or how you waved your hand when you would go.

The music that you listened to at nights,
the presence of your body next to mine,
some holidays, some days when we both cried,
the fights we had, the crossing of the line.

No. None of those things will be on my mind,
I shall not want to think of them at all.
What will stay with me after you are gone,
is darkness, staring at an empty wall.

Don't go before I go as well from here,
your absence is the only thing I fear.

72 The Best Days without You

The best days are in solitude when not with you,
on furniture with cats and books and time,
the worst nights waiting up the stairs for me;
a hungry beast, dark black called lonely wolf.
I don't want to be there under that roof
to listen how the time is ticking distance.
The best days are in solitude when not with you.

73 My Summer Dream

It was a mood I had a while ago,
when nights were warm, sheets moving in a breeze
that brought in scents of flowers so exquise,
I just let my imagination flow.

A violin played somewhere in the street,
a slow and tender tune that filled my mind
with dreams of happiness and love, the kind
that all our weary minds in darkness need.

They mingled with the laughter of the night,
I was in the greenest fields I'd ever seen,
or climbing mountains where I'd never been,
while all around me everything was bright.

The morning greeted me with rain and cold,
and lesser joy than in my dreams was told.

74 Remember

Friends, and your head was resting in my lap.
I wore a dress that summer: blue, pink rose,
and there was sun, but best thing was that you
were resting in my lap and we were close.

Then we made a child to end the summer.
My dress became too tight to wear.
Your head then found another place to rest
from where you kissed the baby, stroked my hair.

Friends, and we watched all our children play,
a new child living in my lap once more,
and at night I rested on your shoulder,
while little feet would come in through the door.

Loud fell the rain in summer nights,
friends came by in shady evening hours,
children grew to leave the house one day
and I still wear a blue dress with pink flowers.

75 Our Fall

Your breath on my face
I watched you sleep, eyes shiver
autumn light caught us
some moments are like that
two minds loving each other
honoured with a smile.

76 Togetherness

I feel you and your thoughts float into mine.
A woven cloth are we together then,
you know exactly of my what and when,
our threads of thoughts always intertwine.

I hold back nothing, when we are alone,
you open up, there are no guessing games,
we watch the birds without knowing their names,
to us the only meaning is their tone.

We try to keep togetherness and such,
when often you and I are far apart,
too far to feel the beating of your heart,
too far to say you matter to me much.

We cherish every moment that we got
together, when we are, and when we're not.

77 Would We Need More

If we could fly away
together, you and me,
and take our needed rest
on a sailing ship at sea,
and find a fish to eat,
would we need more,
would we stay there,
or fly back to the shore?

78 October

I fear the shrinking of the days,
the light that's fading sooner every day.
Colder nights approach me in my home,
and make me shiver in so many ways.

I shall remember better days of warmth
while winter grey and mist surround me tight.
When the lamp is on all hours,
till it's spring, all's dead, no colours and no flowers, too.

So until then I wait for sparks of light,
a candle shiver on a Christmas eve,
a star, a lighthouse beam, a smile,
and once a while a letter sent by you.

79 To Be Silent with This Man

To be silent with this man
keep him company through nights
dream a world that is just ours
maybe happiness is such
to know he is there with me
when the dark enclosures all
to be silent with this man
it is all I need to sleep

80 We Mortal Souls

The universe has nothing to do with the love
we earthlings feel for one another,
hysterical love songs are such lies.

You and I know what love is.
It has boundaries, as we have a mother,
we are no gods.

There are no stars that watch us,
even songs can't make us
be more than
creatures who will die.

But we have love.
Now that is something.
That is enough.

81 Found in Time

Had I found you back, earlier in life,
I would not have known you totally,
nor appreciate the miracle
of our encounter, as I do,
knowing you now.

Had we loved each other but too soon,
I would not have known how to handle.
More confused we would go each our way
another illusion gone, more pain
to overcome.

Had we loved before, being so young,
I would not have realized meaning,
you would have been a sparrow by now,
not eagle, majestic, forever
ruling my sky.

82 Home Isn't an Address

Home isn't an address,
it's a feel that you give,
both your arms inviting,
being where we belong.

It is there in your arms,
as I sleep contented,
a feeling of safety,
being where I should be.

I shall not mind what place
we are staying awhile,
but preferably it's
somewhere close to the sea.

You smile when I wake up
not knowing where we are
but I can hear the roar
and the air smells of salt.

Only together we're home,
knowing each other well,
being ourselves at ease,
no matter where we are.

83 Night Shifts

The busy moment before night I hate as
you make haste for work and leave me by myself,
I watch you dress, and hear you stumble
down the stairs, white light is shining
in the bathroom when I share the cold to see you off,
but I am in the way, no kiss or hug, no time.

The quiet moment before dawn I cherish,
you asleep and near me, close, but now a bit
estrange, as light has not yet found your face.
I watch you in your elsewhere space
that I can never share with you. I love you
deep, in latest moments of the night.

84 The Cave

I lived in your cave, we forgot day and night,
how to eat and to sleep, as the search
for what mattered in life
began there and then.

Heaps of books we ploughed through, we yelled, fought, forgot.
Making up with much wine to drink.
And in this cave we made love,
we made our first child.

He now is a mate, on a white sailing ship,
so we did well, considering all.
We both lived more, together,
finding our reason.

Once I lived in your cave where the truth was born.
We explored all in true honesty
and it was there in the cave
that we became us.

85 A Romance

When we were together
in the moist and moulded bunker,
the rain fell down through leaking holes
and poured on us to wash away this sin.

You took a feather
from the dead dove.
I remember very well
you wrote your name on me
with this feather on my skin
and with every stroke you wrote
I was more yours than I would ever be,
had it been written there with fire.

You engraved your name in me
with the feather, without trace,
with every touch and thought. With love.

In our embrace we spent the night
and the candle that we had, shone a
trembling yellow light
on concrete walls with swastikas.

There I was your bride.

86 Bride

Bright,
as if it had never been here before
the light after a lovemaking hour
was peeking through the curtains, kissed your face
but you slept on, breathing calmly, your pace.

You turned, while I went to take a shower
only to come back, sleep with you once more.

Now,
light slowly leaves us alone to rest.
Your arms around me, I hear your heart beat,
a reminder that all this will go too,
but it is hard thinking of losing you.

I have to forget mortality, need
to think of the now, and hope for the best.

Bride,
is the word, and I was, I will be
your bride, in the morning, the night, the day
if you'll have me, forever I shall be
your bride, and you will be lover to me.

Now sleep, I will wait, in my dreams anyway,
till you come for more loving, gratefully.

87 Magic Time Between the Sheets

That magic time when real is mixed with fake
as dreams have overtaken truth once more,
and every fictive bend is in the make,
yet we believe that we were here before,
some cities dangerous and strange appear
with streets to wander in while getting lost,
there is no telling if the end of it is near:
the purpose of these nights is to exhaust.
But once in a while the dreams will take us there,
to places full of paradise delight
with waterfalls and flowers everywhere,
and this is time when we enjoy the night.
Some hours we may spend between the sheets
away from trouble and from other's needs.

88 Dance

For a moment I danced with you,
it was outside and there was rain,
the music drifted off with the showers
but this moment was ours, our heaven
that will remain in dark clouds above us.

89 Proper Dancing in the Light of the Fridge

First time we met
it was not exactly a tango,
it was no dance at all,
it was running across town,
in and out all taverns.

Starting our relation,
we started with nothing
but what we wrote in our letters,
and our bodies came closer
on the floor where a mattress made a bed.

Now so many years later
we do an occasional waltz
quietly together,
we don't need music
in each other's arms
in the kitchen at night.

You and me, I love you
so what if it's a cliché,
it's what I feel,
as I know you now
enough to dance
a waltz in the light
of the fridge.

90 Hospital Room

You enter the room and a drip, or is it a bomb, starts to beep,
a hunchbacked nurse runs in to replace the antibiotics while
outside it is starting to snow red snow,
somewhere in the hospital someone is crying in Chinese characters
that are spread over the walls
as ambulance sirens approach and go right through the ceiling,
a dog is barking with an increasingly higher voice
till it sings an aria from Carmen,
and all I know is that you enter the room.
I never felt more serene. All is well. Let me sleep now.

91 Vintage

We could argue with words,
bare footed, smashing grapes
to make wine between our toes,
splashing the purple juices
over our white clothes,
jumping up and down,
crushing the fruit.
We could argue like that,
you and I, but the result
was always a good vintage.

No it's not lonely to be here alone in
a bed of marbles, pillows made of stone and
I feel no cold nor do I shiver much
remembering your hands and touching.
No it's not lonely to be here alone at all.

You could always lift me
pregnant as I was
even up the stairs.
No I don't miss you,
not every day,
only when it is time
to yield the fruit,
to smash the grapes,
to make good wine.
We were good vintage.

92 Every Time Again

We find each other
every time again,
in hours we should sleep
I find your arms
and then the rest of you
slowly turning over, too,
as the time again
is ours, we should keep
this finding
every time again.

93 Sea Meets Ocean

There are seas with names
but no one knows where they become oceans,
their waves move on
crossing that imaginative line.

We whispered each other's names
we have moved from sea to ocean;
you became a bit of me
and I'm a piece of you now.

Our shells will wash ashore beaches
to join many others,
all proof of the silent fusion
that happens under the surface.

94 We Are Between Walls

You walk towards and nearer
your feet not making haste,
I know your eyebrows rise
opening the door
to let you in this wall.
Again and more so
deeper
until morning.
So naked can you be
and still not seen
and still not heard
and still alone
in a crowd
or a bed.
Behind the walls live other people.
Other lives walls leave behind.
Where are we when the door is closed?
Your entrance has amazed me.
Over and over again, it is
you entering me until morning
and still you don't see me leave
towards, to be inside, the wall.

95 Understanding

I tried to understand you in words,
in gestures
and how you acted
but I only got the shell of you,
the shattered, battered shell.
I could never get any deeper
than the surface,
the outside,
the façade,
till that moment on the rainy beach,
were we walked out a fight in bitter silence,
when you turned round to face me,
to say that you were scared
to lose me
too.

I never loved you more
and never would love you less
in the future
that now almost is our past.
Because in that moment
I understood you
for always.

96 Come Home Tonight

When you do come home tonight
let me light the big fire,
the candles shall greet you so
please do come home tonight.

We will drink hot cocoa,
get the blankets on the floor,
the candles will be shining all evening
and the winter forgotten,
just do come home tonight.

97 Breathing Your Love

Breathing without thought your love,
like air on crispy winter mornings
when geese are calling loud above our heads,
my awareness of the better now awakes.
I find this peace in being close to you,
in breathing without thought,
this is enough, this is enough. This is
the moment I have sought.

98 The Light for Evening Eyes

I see you in the light for evening eyes,
when daylight's done and candles shine near you.
The sharpness of the day that wants no lies
is gone, now rules another sort of true.
I hear you speaking lower than in day
as if the dark outside has urged you to
be quiet for the danger that well may
be threatening our splendid time for two.
Those evenings spent with you in gentle pace
is all I need to make me leave the day
with nothing needed, and nothing to do,
just watching you, your eyes, your evening face
while light is fading, no more words to say.

99 Storm

I watch the sad clouds move over the sea
while sand is blowing you out of my mind.
I'll worry no longer of what has been
but go with the gulls that fly in the storm,
onwards, away and forever myself,
and the golden sun is returning now.

Trying to forget I am lost here now,
I'm standing near the black turbulent sea
thinking how much there still is in myself
that I don't know, discovering my mind.

On and on waves are rolling in this storm.
I walk on, to where I have never been.
We could have had love, and we could have been
together, watching these gulls leaving now,

see them flying bravely towards the storm.
We'd sit on a dune thinking of the sea.
Not a worry, not a care on my mind
and I could have had you all to myself.

But I am not here now to think of myself.
Pondering over all that might have been,
I decided you are gone from my mind,
so why should I keep wanting you here now
as if it would be: you, me, and the sea
both sheltering in your coat from the storm.

To blow away these thoughts I searched the storm
but I can't always keep fooling myself
this is what was whispered over the sea:
It was in vain, I never should have been
here, thinking I was over you by now,
as the truth is you haven't left my mind.

Just as I am starting to doubt my mind,
a man . . . you walk towards me in this storm
and you spread both your arms to hug me now.
You know me better than I know myself
and knew this was the place I would have been.
Your coat around us both, we watch the sea.

100 Back

We walked before here, hand in hand then,
see how much the sea has taken since.
The beach was wider, remember when
we swam here in a ritual rinse.

You throw a memory at me in smile,
my senses seem to waken from a sleep
that has been keeping me a timeless while
from living in the highest and the deep.

Seagulls witness how we slowly start
to walk faster than we did for long.
Though running in the cold waves is not smart,
we are both back, right where we belong.

101 My Flowers for You

Flowers can be that, loving colours,
living in a meadow no one sees them,
where no one has ever been,
still giving all,
till death takes them away.

I want to find flowers never seen,
from within my mind to say
I would not be alive without you,
but just a body with no source nor goal,
some homesick bones travelling in skin.

102 In Love

In love with all I sense around me,
that was already here, waiting patiently
until I had sense enough to feel
how rain could clean me,
wash away cluttered neglect,
I know it's real:
in this love with life I feel reborn.

Outside I hear the storm, the sea;
to me, when I was much forlorn,
it was unknown that all this
waited there for me.

While I was none aware,
my senses must have grown,
subconsciously
and they no longer hide now.

I feel you think of me,
my hands reach out to get the phone,
a moment later it does ring, and it is you.

Through the moving curtain
a scent of tar is blown in by the wind
from a ship that has long gone.

Life comes to me as I'm grounded on my feet
and certain of the things I've done.
I know love now as I am in it.
All of me, I am surrounded.

103 Footsteps

It was morning, not yet day though
when I noticed snow had fallen.

And outside reminded nothing
of the past days, all was white now.

Some fresh footsteps had your shoe size,
I got thinking they were your marks.

The next morning snow was melting,
your impression became water.

Gone the winter, I'll keep waiting
for the morning when I see you.

104 Before It Happened

Once, time meant none to us, was just a phrase
we didn't know about. We were together on the beach
and felt the wonder of this place, our secret heaven.

In silenced golden light, awaiting changing of the weather,
we found a sort of peace, a moment lasting our lifetime.

A storm was soon to come, but in this dreamed eternity,
just before the dark took over, I was one in thought with you,
our bodies one as well, unknown there would be a goodbye
that could not be avoided.

I don't remember now how long we stayed upon that beach.
The first rain fell, while in the village, the church bell started ringing,
to warn of danger and of flood. The storm began and damaged all.

When the night gave up to hide its shame,
it was revealed as well that you were gone.

Searching in the sand, I only found the faded contours of your name,
and, washed ashore among the debris of the storm,
was time to think of once, and us,
the way we were before it happened.

105 Love Secrets

It rained all day, it was a cheap hotel.
Well enough for our brief encounter,
a bottle of wine and two plastic cups.
We watched the seagulls mate, this view from our
window made us unable to make love,
we laughed as the birds went on like their
life depended on it. It did somehow.
You nicked the towel as a souvenir.
Now we both know seagulls do it smiling
and that you have heaps of hotel linen.

106 We

We might make it as a couple;
for the moment we don't care,
unaware of time we're sharing,
hours, dreams, the days and nights,
unaware we leave the plural
far behind us, far away
as the we becomes a one.
As if gravity is done.
It's in your touch. In what we say.
We might make it as a couple;
for the moment we don't care.

107 *With You*

When I'm with you something happens to the sky:
two birds appear, they carry straws to build a nest
and clouds collide above us, the horizon is fading.

Earth is not a solid truth, not our ground any more,
a shadow, always a good place to hide, now flies,
no longer gives me shelter. Words surround us

in songs that come from passing cars, and the names of books
are sequels to our talk. You say there is a sign in all of this.
When I'm with you I know their meaning.

108 Sensing You

The timbre of your voice is in the sound
the North Sea makes now the wind turned west,
and shells in fancy shades are washed ashore,
along with driftwood sculptured by the salt;
the deepest green and brown of seaweed, all
neglected presents, the beach indifferent
of gulls mourning over loss. I hear you
in every wave that falls apart in foam.
I pick the shells, stone flowers to take home.

109 Your Return

In the crowd I saw you
straight and tall, like always
slower than the others
coming from the train; I
had to smile as I saw you
approach me in slow motion.
You wore your coat, the blue one,
still without the torn off button.
I knew what had caused its departure.

Maybe attraction can't be told
from the speed of reunion,
from the smiles we send each other
or from the flowers we get.
It is in what is absent on arrival
after a long time of missing,
what seems to have gone into oblivion,
but has not; what has been a precious item
and is now living in my pocket.

110 When We Were There

Thin moments gone forever
reflect falsely in what we saved and unfold:
the shine of a postcard of the place in summer
while we were there in winter
and the light was greyish.

Cliffs and rocks caught our attention
and the smell of a foreign meal,
but gulls of the kind we knew
reminded us that we were not there forever.
The sunset washed ashore to die at our feet.

I found a writing pen with the ink dried up
but it had such lovely colour, teal,
and you captured sounds from that place,
they danced on your tongue in a pirouette,
only to jump ship the moment we left Britain.

111 Doing Nothing

All I want to do is be here
while I wait for the shadows
doing nothing but love you
your voice and your mind,
intertwined with my mind, in my voice,
with my hands and my eyes
in your eyes and your hands,
from a distance,
miles above life,
while I wait for the shadows
that grow from behind the cherry tree
to follow my thoughts,
live them, let blood run through my veins
while I wait for the shadows
that grow from behind the cherry tree,
slowly covering all of those thoughts
in forgetful darkness.

112 Ritual

You move in me and I hold you
as simple is the nature call.
We even made some children
while we did it.
A ritual to please the pope,
to give all schools a bit of hope,
to reproduce, to be intimate strangers.
We make love, we break it too,
we destroy and build again,
and flesh on flesh the time goes by,
a whisper, scream, a mournful cry,
a little death before a life begins anew.

113 Sinking Oyster

We went lost more often in such nights
where lights were only sending us astray.
But this was different, no sea was ever vaster.
Like a closing oyster shell forever sinking
deeper from the surface and from me
your love went down and all the salt
there is, comes from my tears. Not from the sea.

114 Certain of a Hug

What is certain? The word does not reflect
anything, like: money, will you be there,
nor sunshine. Health. I am not so certain
that we shall be here tomorrow evening
but let's assume. Assume is good, makes sense.
If we are still here tomorrow evening,
same sofa, with us watching the weather,
let us hold each other tight, let us hug.
We made it through another day. Shall we?

115 Why Little Flies Drown

After a while that summer you wanted to find us a place
where we could do more than talk.
A hotel would have been obvious, but we had no money.
You knew someone who owned a summer house though.
We didn't make it to the bed, the view
of the sea and the taste of the retsina
where little flies choose to drown
—the wine was so sweet they gave their lives
for a sip—kept us on the veranda.
The sun went down faster than I had ever seen
and we held hands knowing each other,
not understanding the choice of little flies that drown.
Years later I went back there. The summer house
was gone for the most part, though there were traces left
of the veranda. Sand had covered the floor boards.
I sat there thinking how it all had been,
the ride here on the back of your rented bicycle,
and that the sun went down so fast that night,
and I opened a bottle of wine I brought with me.
Retsina. Out of nowhere they came,
little flies. With no hesitation they entered the bottle,
sure of a quick death. And they were right.
I felt your presence while the evening gave me
one more sunset, faster than I had ever seen.

116 As You Sleep (And Wake Up)

I look at you as you are asleep in your chair,
and I cry, for no other reason than my thoughts.
I notice how you hair is whiter now.

What if I am gone before you, who will laugh with you,
share your dark sense of humour, and who will be there
watching you sleep in your chair?

I cannot die before you do.
Watch me care, watch me age as I watch you.
And stay here. Care for me.

From outside a silence comes.
My eyes closed, I drift away
and meet you in a dream.

We run across a beach into a sea
where we make love and swim away from all of it
together. Hand in hand.

We both awake, you smile. You had a dream,
you say. You dreamt of making love again,
not remembering where. It was with me though.

You are convinced of that. I know exactly where it was,
as I just came from there. Your hand is reaching out for mine.
Some dreams come true, more so than others do.

117 *What Will Remain*

What image will remain
in latest thoughts of life
when everything has been,

will it be an image
of meadows where we ran,
of sea that gave us peace,
or will it be that of the face
we knew and loved?

With eyes already closed forever,
I shall hope to think of you
and go distracted, not alone.

118 The Mastodon in the Room

This loving you is not about me now.
When I don't see your eyes nor feel your ways
it's present in your absence where somehow
it turns up as a mastodon who stays.

I see its eyes at night, before I fall asleep,
it groans so friendly while others ignore
the fact it's in the room, a love so deep
perhaps cannot be dealt with anymore.

The hunters that are luring just outside
and want to kill my mastodon of love.
They have no chance, it knows in time to hide
from them. This love and I find this enough.

The last of its species may this love well be,
but it is mine. It is the love of me.

119 Let This Present Be Continuous

Morning light touches the kitchen table,
memories of the night before
are dancing in the dust,
ending in the glass you raised
to drink to lust and loving
in the present continuous tense.

I don't want to think of the future.
We'll continue our love with this present.
I sense you in the morning dust
that never falls down
but stays dancing in sunlight
over yesterday's wine.

120 As the Moon Does

Few items mean so much to me as the moon does, or
a sunrise, a pet's photo, smiles with crackling lines,
the smell of tea, contours of old castles. Cathedrals,
relieve after a storm, surviving all.
Clean sheets. Our family. Standing by the sea.

A hand on a shoulder. Our sons. Your letters.
The silver and green shamrock hanger I got in Dublin.
A Christmas tree. That happy feeling on a ship.
To be alone. Write. Read, or days in May. Violins.
New notebooks. Your body, and the verb to be.

Chocolate and train trips, walking, old cities, Norway.
Perfume, days after giving birth, getting published.
That I can see. A good bed after a long day. Fresh morning air.
Daisy chains, sweet white wine, an April shower.
The blue of the sky. Snow maybe. Sense of being free.

121 My Man

You came to my bed
through my heart and the door,
through walls of my fortress,
my battles and fears.

We shed tears and we shared,
fell, stood up,
but we learnt.
And now
you snore in the mornings.
I listen.

122 Hearing the Daylight Enter

The quietness is all I'm looking for,
as the noise of butterfly wings flying,
of slow-moving clouds, of the music I
find in your eyes, would be too much already.

Before we slept, the sound of our bodies,
of lips and sheets, of wanting more,
was what I saw and it was darker then.
I felt all senses, they became insane

Have you ever heard the colour red scream
so loud that it would hurt your ears and eyes?
The indigo of night was whispering,
and I watched how you slept beside me.

Silenced by the night, enough, I listen
how the daylight enters softly our room.
That is all I want to hear right now,
only that, to wake you up. My love.

123 Searching for Your Socks

Give or take, a few oddities,
then I can deal with that.
Even with your socks everywhere
in impaired numbers, I am shy.

So many years of searching perfectness,
we still ended up together.
And I still don't know you,
nor where socks go after they must die.

124 Dream

I dreamt: of your arm around my shoulder
as we stood high upon the dune
and we were both watching yesterday
sink in the fire of hell, where it belonged.

So much older was the world that day.
Tomorrow had to wait another night
but your arm was around my shoulder.
If future had a feel, then this was it.

125 Waiting for an Owl

I waited longer than I wanted to
for our sign to show up in the woods,
a sign we had agreed on, you and me,
on your death-bed of green linen tree leaves.

Exactly then, when I would think of you,
an owl was to appear and say the word.
Magic might be possible for lovers.
I waited. Then I thought of you so strong.

But there was silence when I said your name,
before I heard the caw above my head.
So like you to send me a crow instead,
a mile too far and minutes overdue.

126 Don't Regret Me

When I am dead, please think of me once more,
not as the wife that faded into grey,
with eyes too tired, lips too thin to say
the farewell words I should have said before.

Think of me once the way I would have been
had I lived on, if so, and you stayed mine.
See me once as our bodies intertwine.
When I am dead, picture me in this scene.

We had a choice and took the one we did;
it was the wrong one, I can now admit.
We didn't know that. We just had enough.

But worry not about what we have done
or said, once I am dead. When I am gone.
It was so worth it to have known your love.

127 Be My Dreamt Reality

I wonder off to where we might have gone,
if words had not been said and deeds not done.
I drift on further from reality
in sepia, in ocean blue, in grey
and always there is you. Please stay some more
so I can ponder, be where we would be;
it was so nice the way we were before.

128 We Age

Let's not forget our age and that it matters,
we cannot climb the cliff the way we could,
and even if we can, should we
pretend that we are younger than our years?
In time forgotten are all names in letters,
that loved ones sent us in some caring mood.

We are like fossils, we are ancient shells,
but even if the bones are aching worse,
and only transport in our future is a hearse,
we must not wait till tide washes our feet.
It is the power that we find inside ourselves
that is our age. The heart that is our beat.

129 Why the Bird Sang

We know why the bird sang
but there is no need to tell others.
Can this be our secret,
a key to the old lock,
(the bird sang just for us
did it not)?

Do you remember that wedding
when we walked around in that park,
all dressed in festive clothes?
We were in a bright sort of heaven,
meeting each other in sunlight with drinks.

This is not why the bird sang.
We might tell so to others
but it would not be true.

Still that wedding of others
where we walked in fine gardens
with a castle nearby
and we all wore white,
was a little like heaven.

If I ever do find you
again at some wedding
in sunlight, or attending
a funeral in the pouring rain,
and the bird sings,
look at me again in that way.
We shall make a new secret
to add to the others.

I can keep a secret,
a little bird told me how
when it sang at that wedding.

130 Pale Blue Walls

Inside pale blue walls with golden framed mirrors,
a room with high ceilings, dusty sunlight is shining
through crystal carafes with ruby coloured port.
Here, who would be unhappy?
A blonde little girl is playing piano, and lazy bloodhounds
sleep at her feet. This is a mansion, but no smell of hunting.
Be here, when you hurt. Be here with whomever
you want to share this. In this room, I am with you, unseen,
reading a red covered book. And I'll peek now and then
to smile in your direction.

131 On the Edge

Those thoughts of what is true, what did you really think, how can we know that of another?
We stood beside each other, and we watched the waves withdraw.
They left me in confusion, were we in love or no more so, could I reach for your hand
and would you take mine in yours, too? So much I longed to feel your warmth, to smell the leather of your coat. Instead I started walking on.
After more time than I could bear, I knew you followed me when I heard your breathing.
For a mile I didn't dare to look at you, we had not said a word, this silence had come so between us, louder than the sea. We stared over the beach. A frozen moment; it was ebb. From now on, everything could happen.
And then I felt that arm around my shoulder. All was cleared without ever being spoken out.
A seagull screamed surprised over our heads, and in your smiling eyes was love. Those thoughts of what is true, we need not know it of each other.
The sea came back as we went on with life, and walked away. Together.

132 Stranded on a Sand Bank

He touches my hand and then his book,
thinking of other things I guess
than of my hand and of his book,
his eyes drifting away. 'Tis fine,
as long as I am at his side, why speak?
Why say what's obvious, why look?

Our boat has stranded on a bank,
we should get dressed maybe,
we need to catch the tide.
I want to feel his skin on mine.
I see the water in the setting sun,
the water's bleak. Goodbye has just begun.

Part 3
When All Falls Apart

Poems 133-194

133 Starting the End

There was fog, making it even worse to go
as I sort of disappeared, I felt
lost before you even woke up
and looking back was no use;
the house was gone. For a while
I was nowhere in particular,
except in between two lives,
the one with you and the one after you,
and there was no fading to make it bearable,
only blind walls of grey indifference,
of moist that silenced all,
though each of my steps
was a meteor landing.

134 The Stranger You Became

The more I knew you, the stranger you became
who lived between my sheets but not to stay
the night. My lover whom I knew by name
and body, but whose soul was always under way.

135 I Shall Not Rage

Once more the mirror puts me in my place
while skin is trying hard to camouflage
what's left of once my body now I age,
but see, I shall not rage, I shall not rage.
Never mind the hollow eyes that stare at me,
and follow me in bitter silenced spite
across the room, where clothes and blankets lie
about our love. The mirror tells me why.
Still, when you come at nights and find me here
regret me not, forget me not. Love me.
I shall not understand you and your choice,
as long a whisper will be in your voice.

136 The Way You Say My Name

A sadness in your shoulders as we walked
makes me aware of how the mood is gone.
It has to be something that I have done;
it has been such a while that we have talked.

Essential now is what is on your mind.
Have I done something wrong that I don't know?
The words I want to say have lost their flow.
I stutter while I need to speak refined.

How come your eyes are all that I can see,
when in between us there is bitterness
that's blinding, meaning that you love me less,
the flow of your words say that you agree.

When we shut up at last, you say my name
and all that I have doubted drifts away.
You'll stay. Maybe our lives will be the same.

137 Meeting You in Mist Only

Now we drifted away from each other,
almost out of my horizon you sail.
We pass each other in mist at low tide.

And when we're at home, the house seems bigger,
sometimes we meet in the bathroom mirror,
before the hazing starts to fade us both.

And I still aim for your approval
and I wait for the tide to change,
the mist to go. I wait for our collision.

138 Alone Now

Not much has changed since I was here with you,
the beach has stayed a scene of blowing sand,
under my hand the shells are fragile rocks.
I feel the earth invade my skin and eyes,
one with water, sand, and air I shall live on.
And even if I die now, I'll be part of
all that starts as sky, dividing sea
from land. The shells are fragile rocks, how
slow the waving water takes me over.
But you are gone now, I am all alone.

139 The Read

Living in your sentences for a while
I felt safe, under the roof of your lines,
in cupboards with beautiful cutlery
and china, I found what I was missing.
Every metaphor a new adventure,
I slept on your sofa, held in your arms,
dreamt your chapters, my comforting blankets.
I was part of you and your mind was home.
And now I finished the book, so I have
to move on, feeling homesick already.

140 Repeating Miracle

A miracle cannot repeat itself,
therefore I thought it a onetime affair
to have known you senseless
in the biblical sense
before you left on a ferry in mist
and bitterness.

Then I saw you again unexpectedly,
as we met by chance in a bar
surrounded by smoke
making the air rather dense.
Again you stayed for a while,
followed by another departure forever.

Each day now your eyes reflect
in shop windows, movies
and trains passing by.
Through anonymous faces
in images on busses,
I see miracles happen this way.

141 Our Last Night

On that evening we had decided
that you and I were not meant to be,
but a final walk along the sea
might make the end a bit easier.

You had packed all your stuff already,
and carried your brown suitcase with you,
as if you would step and walk away
over the waves. You looked holier.

We sat, watched our earth move from the day,
the sky went from blue to indigo.
You were still here and I held your hand,
tomorrow was bound to come too soon.

Another day gone, another end.
What mattered most, or what mattered less,
at that moment we had no idea,
only that we bonded with the moon.

You whispered my name like you loved me,
the moon was almost full above us,
we had no time to waste or to spite;
the ferry would take you anyway.

But we made some memories that night,
a ship sailed by in silent movement,
all in our lives seemed meant to be
In spite of so much, you did not stay.

142 Bits and Pieces of You

In bits and pieces you saw my life stuttering through clumsy poems,
my loves as they had been and as they were dreamt,
in the lives of elegant butterflies hopping from flower to flower, or
seen through crows' feathers and in black clouds,
words contemplating over sailing ships on seas of aspiration,
or waving branches of dying trees.
The birds that make their nests
and rain falling to erase the worst of our sorrow
were all substitutes for what I wanted you to know.

Now you have found yourself in there, or so you say,
what more can I do, now we stand to look down
at the leftovers of our affairs in verse.
Yes, it was that deep perhaps, or do you find it shallow
and not always about you? See, there still is a bit of attraction left
if you look through the hairs of the feather.
It was that intense. You understand
and hand me the dustpan and brush to clean up.
While you make coffee in sunlight dust, new lines emerge.

143 Cruelly Faded

The cruellest kind of love
seems one that's fading
from the red of passion
to the pale bleached pink;
not the one that ends
in fights and hatred,
not the letters written
in poisoned ink,
not the love that sheds
so many tears.
The fading love
seems to be the cruellest,
love that slowly ends
over the years.

144 Not Without You

No sunrise is the same, not without you.
Sometimes I feel an anger in the sky,
at times the light is calling all a lie
to paint me pink and gold when I am blue.

No evening has the scent of sweetness now,
as if all flowers died the day you left,
like love was stolen from me, this is theft.
Where to begin my life anew and how?

One day the light maybe will make more sense,
when I am over you, but shall I be
the very same that was the I in we,
if I can only think in the past tense.

Just now I settle for a dream of you
to get me through the night in dark and cold,
without your arms around me, who will hold
me now forever, what will get me through?

No sunrise is the same, not without you,
to paint me pink and gold when I am blue.

145 No Postage

I kept the postcard that you sent to me,
but that is all that is reminding me,
there is no more of you to find you in,
there's another now getting your flowers.

I've counted hours that you spent with me
and about now you've seen her more than me.
We had our ending. You a new beginning.
What now is yours and hers, once all was ours.

The card was sent from where we once made love,
reminder that all this was not enough,
that's how I felt about it anyway.
Was it a sign that you remembered some of it?

I shall not frame the card but keep it safe
in a drawer, unseen like an unloved waif.
The card is dear but came with some delay.
I paid a fee. You had not stamped it.

146 Your Space

A place without a view and curtains drawn,
nobody can get in, except by force.
Two doors, that's all we see, but what goes on?
If secrets are a room, then this is yours.

I like to think its walls are red and gold,
it's where you go when you are not with me.
Sometimes I think the smell of it proves mould,
another truth behind these doors maybe.

The truth that isn't about why you go
but more so saying why you cannot stay
lives there. You keep the creature and you know
there is no other option, no such way.

Your truth, the one that you still feed with lies
will live forever as my own surmise.

147 Thinking of You

I was thinking of you
how you looked at me
those eyes of yours
piercing right through me
and I wanted to feel more of you
than a thought
so I placed my hand on the window
where I had watched you leaving
then I noticed
the glass had a crack
as if it was pierced.

148 I Got a Dying Rose

I got a rose, a red one,
she's standing in a vase
where I watch her die
some more each day.

This flower, given out of love,
is making me more sad
as all you felt for me
is dying with her petals.

A plastic rose, a red one,
is what I need to get,
and if I'll close my eyes a bit
we found a love forever.

149 Fading Lunatics

Now I can't hope against all odds,
as all has been. We just go on now.
Me in my life, and so do you in yours.
I don't know why, but we just do our things.

I'm learning how to live a no-hope life.
Sometimes a book page has your coffee stain
and more signs that remain of what we had
are in my head, only come out when I'm alone.

You seem to be doing all right, I'm told.
Maybe I would feel better if you were
miserable too. Your coffee stains and me
are fading lunatics, they some more than me.

150 Duvet

We made the featherbed together
and feathers flew around,
they did not touch the ground.
We made our bed and lay in it,
and watched them fly around.

The featherbed is gone,
and now you are away.
I bought me a duvet
but I can't make the bed alone,
I don't know how it's done.

151 Thawing You Away

While thinking of you I came across shapes
never seen before, images in ice,
in clouds. As if all the world wanted me
to remember you in more than the truth.
But ice will melt and clouds will drift away.
Your memory won't find me in the end.
Nothing of what we were about will stay.

152 Farewell

Like a captain on a ship that is about to sink
I see you standing in a mist,
and you have eyes that know.
I think your eyes matter the most. And hands.
The captain stays on board. All others go.

The sea takes all, and closes silently
over the wreck the ship is now.
I see you. The mist is getting dense, but there
you are, a last glimpse and I know you're gone.
We both say a farewell. It is all done.

153 Mist

In the mist I try to find your hand,
before I lose you altogether.
This weather and your silence
intertwine, make me look
for beacons to hold on.

We hear the far away sound, whist_es
of two passing ships, as their signals
echo in the grey. This mist
seems to be here to stay,
but your hand slips from mine.

154 Defrosting You

The ground so frozen can't be soil
for more than burying cold hearts,
the ones of cruellest birds,
the magpies that we saw, that ate their own.

The cries of birds in blacks and whites
in nights where I can't find you in my bed
under our covers, with those red roses on them,
those you liked, make me shiver.

You are outside now. I wait for winter to move on.
Maybe I'll find you under layers of snow.

This frozen land though will be melting soon,
and death will go.
I touched your face before you went, I kissed your hand.
You have been dead to me before. Your breath came back
like smoke. It will come back again.
So much I have achieved. So much more than you know.

The frost is coming to its end.

155 Thinking You Away

I tried to think you away reason by reason
but you always showed up in my dreams anyway.
In my coffee you floated, in every season,
you always came back, haunting me, day by day.

I then locked my memories of you in a jar
and threw them away in the deep of the sea.
But how I tried, I failed to throw you very far,
you would wash ashore, and always came back to me.

It is fine, as I found a way to compromise:
from five till six in the morning is time for you
but only then I think of you, before I rise,
and before the shower runs, I no more do.

156 I Write You Down

I write you down on paper and in laptop screen
and every word I feel you watching me,
I am more naked than I've ever been
and more alone than I shall ever be.

My words describe not much: in every scene
the hollow stare your eyes were, nights when we
had just made love, and made me feel obscene.
I am more naked than I've ever been.

I write you down so you will leave my mind,
but every line is bringing you to me
in serendipity, in thoughts I find.

157 Not That I Think of You That Much

I found a dead goose on the beach,
the one that wouldn't make it to the South,
where you live.

It's body was still warm, eyes open.
in disbelief the end had come.
Small feathers trembled
as in an attempt to fly;
like you never giving up.

My hands dug a grave in the wet sand
while in the distance,
over mournful evening waves,
against the blood of the sky,
the other geese came back in silence.
You would have loved that sight so much.

I felt their wings move air above me.
then they went,
a V-formation with one empty place.
The sea covered the grave
and I ran home, a feather in my hand,
to write this letter for you.

Not that I think of you that much.
Only when I see a dead bird,
that was southward bound.

158 Lost without You

Lost in the mist, I stood still for a while.
The foghorn everywhere, the rest was silent,
what can you sense when sound and sight seem gone:
I heard the mist, a softly cloud drop drip
on dead pine tree needles all around me
and louder it became, my ears made them
your name, my eyes now saw your face in grey,
a hand as well. Maybe it was a tree
that showed me how to walk and find my way,
and I heard not your name, but only dripping.
But lost in mist, I've sensed you for a while.

159 Reunion

You are there somewhere in this same room, this local concert hall
that is almost demolished,
that's a cathedral
built for gods,
tonight.

The smell of rain coats and tobacco mingles with your scent.
I know it is your scent.

I feel your eyes heating up the skin of my neck,
where my white shirt starts,
the India shirt that you liked so much.

That tremble of your forehead vein,
it must be resonating now with the two violins
that are in practice before the concert
and I can hear your heart beat
over that of the testing drum
across the noise of two hundred
shuffling feet and some friendly conversation.

How does it feel for you to see me now,
after the break-up in the snow,
the others, the quarrel, the phone call.
So much has passed in time,
and time fades all sharp edges,
even if you want them to stay sharp,
you sharpen them on a stone,
to feel deeper pain of love, I know
how you like to suffer, feel
impossible love, you find it romantic.

I do want to forgive. If you do, too.
Yes you are there somewhere.
We need to talk perhaps, or better
not.

We all take seats,
the conductor lifts his arm.
Now all is silent
just before the music starts,
that moment in between
expectation and outburst in crescendo,
I turn around and in slow motion
see the back of your head
while you leave again.

The concert starts.
A deadly noise is overtaking the evening.
The roof falls in, the earth opens, all is forlorn
and I die before the end of first session.

160 Dark Season

I watch my life grow darker now each day
and all around me lesser world is seen,
a bitter cold and storms till it is May
a window with no view, a misty street,
my mind that's waiting but for what indeed.

The postman lost a letter no one needs
it's flying high above the neighbour's roof,
forgotten words that no one ever reads
as rain has washed away the ink, they're gone.
The postman sighs and struggles, moving on.

I'm not that good in seasons with no light.
If I could just fast forward a few months,
or replay summer—I would be all right,
relive a bit of magic that I found.

But such is life, to live it all year round.

161 If Only I Could Be Inside Your Thought

If only I could be inside your thought
to alter it a bit for understanding,
make windows in it, have a candle lit,
and fill it with new furniture and plants.

To alter it a bit for understanding
of how it is that I did what I did,
I would just shift the tables and the chairs,

make windows in it, have a candle lit,
because I care to make you see my point,
I would so much be with you in your house

and fill it with new furniture and plants.
If only I could be inside your thought,
make windows in it, have a candle lit.

162 Being Apart

More often when you are not here with me,
I sense you in the way the raindrops fall
right near me, rhythm that explains it all,
but not why you are not right here with me.

Near me, the water falls apart in parts
that splash against my feet, my skin, my hair,
reminding me of days we didn't care
about goodbyes nor raining that now starts.

More often when you are not here with me,
the loss we didn't feel then, comes in parts
of splashing raindrops, and that's how it starts
to be reality, the truth to me.

Near me I sense you close to skin, my hair
and in the rhythm when the raindrops fall.
No. I do not want to explain it all.
For me it is enough to know you care.

163 Finest Moments

Years go on in seasons forever,
never, no never time is in reverse,
over and over we find life is newer,
over and over, eternal rehearse.

The touch of a word, the smile of a melody,
over and over we hang on to these,
never no never shall we fail to increase
our finest collection of such moments each.

164 Past Perfect

There is a stitch on your pullover torn;
like all the clothes that you have ever worn,
I can't throw it away. It's here to stay,
imperfect as the best things always are.

165 Split Second of Mazarine Blue

Mazarine blue is your colour, like the name of the butterfly. I said so when we were still holding hands. When we met again, it was by surprise, in the rain, in a busy street. I saw you first, I think, not sure it was you, we hadn't stayed friends, so I kept walking in the opposite direction of you, wearing my mask of anonymity. The rain caused the smell of dogs and ginger, memories of our last days together, did you smell it too, in the coats of passing by people preventing us from stopping, you did slow down a bit. Your pace is heavier now, older and more determined, but you still wear that Mazarine blue coat with that stain under the collar. And she was walking beside you in red.

Hit by your closeness, I almost ran after you, not bare footed like in my fantasy of our reunion for years, but in green rubber boots, and my hair sticking on my face. I wanted to scream: "I still have your shell, thank you, come back!"—the shell I always keep in my pocket for good luck, cherishing it and carefully keeping it from breaking but I didn't, as you already walked on. Did your eyes scare, laugh, surprise themselves, too? I turned my head away from you, hiding my tears in the rain, not too soon to feel you looked back. My coat wasn't warm enough anymore, I ran home. The light was blinking on the phone, but I didn't answer, deleted the message. To hear your voice now (it was you) would have been unfair. Unbearable. My wet hand accidentally crushed our precious fragile shell and blood started to warm my fingers. You still look so well. Mazarine blue is your colour.

166 A Blanket of Seaweed

A blanket of seaweed was its presence,
that I found on the beach
and tried to spread over the sand.
It waved on a breeze coming in from the sea.

It was light to me, colour and weight,
more friend than ever friendship was.
It covered me, sheltered me for a moment
but as the wind turned east,
getting colder, stronger,
I was not strong enough.

I let it slip out of my hand, it went
somewhere far across the water,
it disappeared. It was your love.

167 There Was a Comma Between Us

There was a comma between us, our names
on the contributor's list in the book,
done so for alphabetical reasons,
there we were,
only divided by interpunction.

Two years after our break-up it was, when
in that bookshop, I bought an eraser.
While her eyes seemed to know what my plan was,
the assistant peeked over my shoulder.
The comma erased, we both took a look.
The result was a stain. I closed the book.

168 Enough to Wish You Well Forever

We then were so alive it seemed unreal,
the beach that night where we were all alone,
and shared a solid feel of trust
there on a dune.

We sat under a full round moon
and then, over the quiet sea,
a boat with all lights on just sailed away,
it had a band on board that played
a Klezmer tune.

We watched it disappear,
the festive ship,
the moonlit sea, a scene so fine
as we had never seen before.

How close I felt to you
and that we were so one
in what we sensed, and there was more.

I don't know where you are today, nor what this life
has given you, but in that night I loved you so,
enough to wish you well forever.

It seemed unreal,
it wasn't. I won't forget it. Never.

169 Forgotten by My Heart

It was forgotten by my heart
that you had loved me then and there,
as we have been so long apart.
How will I know if you still care?

That you had loved me then and there,
the way we parted was so hard,
you left no traces anywhere.

As we have been so long a part
of memories we couldn't share,
and soon you'll stand here well and smart,

how will I know if you still care?
It was forgotten by my heart
that you had loved me then and there.

170 Souvenir

So now you notice me
in wallpaper shadows,
in the cups in the sink
and the laundry in the dryer.

Tomorrow, I think,
my shadow will be gone,
the dishes done.
I will leave my laundry though,
so you will have items
to remember me by
and how it was in bed. And besides,
it is not all completely dry
just yet.

A moment has no measure
I recall some endless seconds,
but time is a given spoil sport,
we count away precious time.

I recall some endless seconds,
waiting for news either good or bad.
Some moments last forever

but time is a given spoil sport,
we invented the word,
now we have to keep pace.

We count away precious time
captivated in hours, minutes, seconds
and never. Always, forever.

171 Fading

More and more our history is fading
into fragments of the past
glued to a butterfly wing, and resting
in the eyes of your framed picture.

The button of your coat
—the one you wore on the beach
and I already don't remember
the colour of that coat—
will lose its meaning.

There will be a day
our history together
has disappeared in the place
between the sea and the sky.

It was navy blue, and it was September.

172 The Hand You Touched Mine With

The hand you touched mine with,
felt warm.
Your blood kept you warmer
than mine did for me
when we were on the beach,
so I warmed myself with your warmth,
you even gave me your sweater.

Now your cold eyes make me shiver again.
Nothing will make me feel better.
The hand you touched mine with,
it will not warm me now
as you won't reach out.
Not like that day
when you gave me your hand
and your warmth on the beach.

173 Politely Stabbed

I was with you in thoughts when I was cooking
when I ate when I drank when I slept
and everything in between.
I never wept, it felt
like you were here looking
over my shoulder.
You were everywhere
in my mind and my body,
though your absence lingered
in the choice of my clothes.

On the pillow the folded impression of you
stared at me till the cat took your place,
I tried to dry the rose you put in my hair
but it moulded, I wore your sweater,
keeping your scent with me,
faking your presence.
I felt your hands when I was alone at nights.

And now we meet again and we dine
and you ask how I am.
I lie that I am fine.

Politely, with every cut
in the steak au poivre
you stab me to pieces.

174 Every Kind Syllable Hurts

Your letters tell me you are well
and to make sure I understand
there are some drawings from your hand
of flowers and of churches, too.
The words are chosen with much care
and all of this makes me aware
this is no longer you at all.

Your letters tell me nothing's well
between the lines I read goodbyes,
I see your honest, caring eyes
and how you struggle to find ways
of letting go in friendly words
but every kind syllable hurts
this is no longer us at all.

175 *What We Never Said*

After awhile, the conversation ends as we are done with speech,
with nothing more to say, there is some time to kill,
so silently we walk on, side by side over the beach,
to dwell in past and present with the tide,
and no more talking taking place,
this will be our way to say farewell. My friend, the ferry waits for you.

Watching you sail away, I'm thinking of the gaps I should have liked to fill.
Perhaps it's so that words mean more to us than normally they do,
when they remain unsaid? As if unspoken they might add some truth?
I don't know if it mattered, still.

176 Departure

After your departure, it was different in the house
where daylight seemed to stay a certain grey.
The heater broke, the doors that wouldn't stay ajar
fell loudly in the lock each time a bit of air came by
and all your letters flew out of the window towards clouds.
The day of your departure, you were gone, away, too far.

177 Sense

When you look outside, is it cold we both see?
Can we hear the sadness,
feel the pain of the half cut tree there?
We should have listened to what colours tell us;
I didn't see where music took you to,
nor did you sense my joy in books I read.
But now. Now that we can look further.
Sense the world, live till the outmost.
Look outside now, feel it all.
I see cold, do you see it too?

178 Absence of You

I'll feel you no longer as part of me,
the nights will be colder and the sun will be gone,
meanwhile in nature everything will move on
towards the new season, as it should be.
The pain of plastic
seen in purest snow
on a winter's day,
cruel and crispy flickering
the pain of plastic
seen in purest view.

My arms will feel heavy without holding you
in evenings when the demons come to play,
I shall miss the calming words you used to say.
Is this just when, or shall I always do?

The cold of plastic
felt in purest snow
on a winter's day,
indifferent of my skin
the cold of plastic
in the purest ice.

A morning will come when you are gone at all,
out of my mind, my body and my heart.
I won't be looking for another start,
your absence starts my season, my true fall.

179 Winter Reflection in Dark Windows

I want to be in winter in a warmer room,
forgotten books are there, a pen and paper sheets.
No one shall enter for a while, I am alone,
and hear how hail and snow play havoc in the streets.

I read and close my eyes to dream away my time,
forgotten names, no faces, it has been too long.
No memory of details, how it ended soon,
I come across that darkest feeling of all wrong.

In winter I shall feel my pain once more this way,
forget it then and bury it in frozen ground.
Inside is comfort of an easy chair that waits,
it is the place where I shall be till I am found.

180 In a Storm

The trees bend in their waving dance,
it is a storm that makes them grow.
It is my chance to be like trees
when I'm in storms so much like these,
and, as those branches, I won't break,
I shall be stronger. I can take.

181 Listen Now

My whispers follow the waves over sea
as they humbly return where they came from,
taking my thoughts and my hopes far from me.
Can you hear what I said where you are now?

Hear the grumbling grouse of the sea over there
listen to all I was trying to say
after our meaning together it's fair.
Whispers are all that remain of our love.

182 Joy

Some rivers end up in a desert land,
not all of them can reach the sea;
the water dried up miles before the coast.

Some lovers never make it as a pair,
together they are worse than on their own;
the love is gone when egos meet their match.

Some trees will never grow full length,
and birds will never build nests in their arms,
but when so, sea and love and birds are joy.

183 Silent Goodbye

We could whisper and let our breath be words;
our hearts would hear their meaning anyway.
Although there's less and less we'd have to say,
we know that goodbye is, when silence hurts.

Say something, just to get me on my way,
to keep me with you while the ferry goes,
and tears are flowing like sea water flows.
We could whisper then, when I leave today.

We could say goodbye and not make a sound,
promises would freeze, linger in the air,
that you would follow soon, and everywhere
is together, forever we'd be bound.

But silence is the bitter proof of end
when words are not enough to make a mend.

184 The Universe Expands

We live in more worlds at the same time
and for every decision,
a new awareness is made.

We take different roads endlessly
and at every crossing,
another future begins,
a new reality awakens.

Trillions of decisions,
every possibility outlived,
how many galaxies
can you and I alone fill,
just figuring out by trying
the best way for trimming hedges,
which shoes to wear,
or how to remain friends?

185 Encounter in Rain

Moments after rain had soaked my bones and skin
I noticed you across the street.
You decided so to have a look at me at the same time.

And then, I could not speak. It was the moment where in
movies all is starting, or all ends.

It was March, the light already that of spring,
but we felt bitter cold as we stood there,
together, with the road between us. Lovers. Friends.

I imagined how the scent of you
was damping from your coat.

We lacked the warmth now,
and I wondered, did you recall how it had been
when we were lovers?

I think you smiled when my mind blushed unseen,
I didn't dare to watch your face.

You made one step towards me, then
a car came in high speed, a scaring "toot"
and you jumped back into your space.

There was water splashing over you,
you shivered, in deep thoughts again you left for good.
The only thing remaining, was the curving of your neck.

186 Don't Closure Me

don't feel too bad for me
I've seen it coming and
it's not the first time now
I know you have to leave
there's no alternative

and so what the hell
it is not really if
we know each other well
I see that now
so pack your stuff
and shut the door
it's been enough
why wait for more
we'll never blend
were never meant

to be a pair
go anywhere
leave me alone
I shall go on
I've always done

she needs you more
the needy one
it's like before
so go away
no I don't cry

they're bits of dust
got them in my eye
pack all you want
yes I can cope
don't leave your lust

don't leave the hope
don't show regret
don't leave me yet
not yet, don't
go

187 After Her

Then evening comes and you are still the same,
a silhouette behind a window glass.
Today nobody here mentioned your name
and in the dark your face is mirrored blank.

The night is still to come and makes no change,
there's nothing moving in the quiet house.
The bed, so useless to the mind, feels strange
with damp and bigger than a bed should be.

The sound the gas makes and keeps you awake,
while comfort of her scent has left you now,
it is the hissing laughter of the snake,
and morning never comes for your relief.

188 The Lark

On evenings when the shade of silence came
in thoughts and whispered sounds, as nature spoke
about the day, now dark, but silently,
to not disturb our nearly sleeping minds,
on evenings when I felt you think of me,
there always seemed to be a singing lark.

My words to you, unspoken, he sang them
to remember well; when cold turned into
frost, he flew away, no sound he left me.
I knew that he would go to you, tell you
of my evening thoughts, and of my quiet
shades, as my silenced whispers he knew well.

He always did return the other day.
An autumn evening was so calm, I sat
under the tree where now the leaves had gone.
Silence felt more present in the absence
of the singing. My lark lay dead under
the last of fallen leaves. Our love was done.

189 A Wave Called Love

Without the words to tell me my condition
I knew that I was lost. The ship was sunk.
Like sailors, drunk, I simply went in deeper waters.
There was no reason to be
anymore. There was no shore, no ground to land my feet.

I just let go, the stream no longer enemy but friend,
and colours, never seen before, were mine.
This peace would never end, as I had found it
in myself.
Then the tide changed and a wave called love washed ashore.
My life was not the same, the way it was before.

190 We Played House

It feels unreal to see you go
into the grey and yellow morning sky,
through the window that you cleaned
not a week ago,
now I see you through stripes.

I tried to repair your jacket,
in whimsical stitches, sitting on the couch,
while you did the outside of the house.
Your window cleaning and my sewing,
imperfect, but good
for at least a lasting memory
of us keeping house.

Through the blurred glass of the living,
I watch you
touch the jacket's scar,
and you turn around, in awe,
for one last moment.

I think I might have left the needle
in the fabric.

191 No Words Can Give Me Comfort

Words are no comfort to me now in pain,
reminders how it is to lose a friend.
A favourite book that's ruined by a stain,
pine trees of stubborn, never to be bent,

like this it feels, a loss, a grieving, hurt,
due to a sad misunderstanding.
You should have known I never was a flirt;
I know that we are far away from mending.

None of your courting I shall really miss,
I don't care for that much exaltation,
and I am not that eager for a kiss,
only for your love and acceptation.

The time beyond the searching of the soul
shall be my memory of you in peace,
those days when we were not apart but whole.
Though for my heart, this pain it will not ease.

My book has found a place inside the bin.
In love there is no one to really win.

192 I Met You in the Mist

Have we really been so close
once, during nights in summer,
when the sea was sparkled with green
lights, more pretty than the stars?

Was it your breath I felt over my cheek,
did you really tell me with your body
of feelings that we dared not speak
and remained unspoken?

Now you are losing hair, that precious hair
I loved to stroke, and those eyes are telling me
your sadness lives in you forever.

I would have reached out with my hand
for you, but you walked on and faded in the mist,
leaving me in silence, surrounded with the grey
of deep regret.

We met, but never we were more apart.

193 Gone but Still There

I do not want to be a part
of a love that moves no heart
but is only there because it was.

It was, it ended, it is gone,
what is over, that is done.
But you linger in my thoughts
and when you laugh, I feel joy too.

My joy for you
has no reason, makes no sense.
It is gone, but still intense.

194 Summer Storm

A summer storm goes by my house,
over my roof, hitting windows, entering keyholes,
howling with drama, clouds exploding over the island
and the harbour is filled with ships searching shelter.

A summer storm goes through my heart,
over my skin, shivering my bones, revisiting soul,
howling my drama, the hurt is not over,
and your arms won't shelter me much anymore.

A summer storm goes further on
over is turmoil, the tempest, the wave rolls,
moving to calmness, to breathing, to peace,
and again I remain, yet away from it all.

Part 4
When Love is Over

Poems 195-227

195 The Wall—Rondeau

I reached this wall, my road must end
as for a wall I came to stand,
and there is no return for me,
a statue here in time I'll be
now you have stopped being my friend
and I don't know why friendship went,
it is so damaged, can't be mend,
what happened is a mystery,
I reached this wall.
On friendship I should not depend
too much perhaps, but I defend
the right to love and to be free
in choices where you cannot see
my reasons being different.
It ended 'cause of argument.
And we won't bow, there's no more we.
I reached this wall.

196 It Was Not Love That Died

Had we known love before
then I would grieve now
for its loss.
Had there been openings
in doors shut,
in conversations,
then there would have been sadness.

Had we known love before
to share, without grieving
other loves,
we would have made it
passed the boundaries
of mere acquaintances
and passed the threshold
of uneasy sex.
Though there is sadness
because there seems nothing here
in this rained over grave
but a hollow coffin.
And grief allows itself to barge in any time
anyway.

197 The Bubble

I think of you while I am in this odd position,
opposite the window,
my legs in a sort of yoga bend way,
but still relaxed, as I do nothing.
I watch.
Clouds, blue pieces of sky, clouds again.
I do nothing.
My eyes start to water, my legs hurt now.
I won't do anything.
I am not thinking of you, am I?
Clouds go by.
Every shape is your face.
I do nothing.
I feel nothing.
I am getting over.

It is getting darker, but slowly,
and I didn't notice till now.
It is cold.
I have to lift myself up.
Out of this position, away from this window.
The clouds are now moonlit hills.
I have to lift myself up.
The cat needs food.
I can only crawl.
My legs are stung by hundreds of bees.
I grab a pillow and close my eyes.
Over you.
I have to be over you now.
Lift myself up.

I wake up when the sun shines in my face.
And again I think of you.
Another day starts.
More clouds.

198 The Bubble Bursts

I am not here at all.
My body is numb.
I am away for a bit.
Out of myself.
Somewhere nice,
my own world.
I am not here.
Don't look me up,
I like it where I am.
I am in a bubble
drifting away from it all,
coping with your absence.

199 Siren

Maybe it means nothing,
but the moment I see you,
coming down the street,
after turning the corner
and popping back into my life,
the siren starts,
like it does every first Monday
of the month at noon,
for no other reason
than making sure it works.

In its hauling noise
you approach,
still far away,
and there are a few side streets
that you might decide to take
and leave again,
but you keep approaching me,
getting taller,
more and more you,
alarmingly more you.

I can see your face now,
the siren reaches its climax,
you walk faster,
start running
and running and finally
you embrace
her. Not me.

The siren slows down
and I shut the door.
Maybe it meant nothing.

200 Metaphorically Speaking It's Over

Like a lost bird in bitter cold snow,
this feeling I have is, and it won't leave.
Like a song that is waiting
in melody fragments,
cannot explain why you needed to hurt me
when I mistook you for being kind.
Like a joke everyone understands but not me.
Like a word that won't come, or a line that has gone
from the back of my mind.
Like a final false note ending it sadly,
over I mean, it is over and done.

201 Good Morning

More than this I could not give you, it was all
but not enough for you to stay.
Inadequate my love has been,
when I felt deep, you saw me shallow.

This is my shadow, not myself,
I went unseen a while ago,
when the door was not yet slammed,
but slowly started falling in the lock.

My morning after all the years we had
before, is going well though,
still no tears, no suicidal thoughts
at all. Not many.

The bed, half empty, will be filled once more,
with books and papers, cats and food,
and memories of you in scent.
It all is well, the way it ended.

You went no day too soon.
After the years we had before,
this is the morning after.
There are no tears, and this is hell.

202 Even Your Scent Is Gone

So much has gone,
now your scent is done.
It lingered long in clothes and hair,
faded away, molecules drifted
where so much has gone,
your scent is done.

203 Loss

I was naked in my own eyes,
but dressed for winter,
lost in my own way,
yet in a familiar street,
when I looked for you
between the bricks in the wall
of the house where I had seen you once,
in windows reflecting only my hollow face.
I found you years later
in the eyes of my next born child.

204 We Were by Accident in the Same Place

We were by accident in the same place,
a gallery where ancient statues stare.
We moved along and passed forgotten grace.

I saw you enter in a sort of haze,
that I still loved you, you were not aware.
We were by accident in the same place.

So much had happened since I saw your face,
to have a talk seemed only to be fair.
We moved along and passed forgotten grace.

Was love still here, or was this not the case?
To think we almost would have been a pair!
We were by accident in the same place.

I never did forget those passion days,
and never stopped to think of you and care.
We moved along and passed forgotten grace.

I wished you'd told me how to keep your pace,
such feelings after so much time is rare.
We were by accident in the same place.
We moved along and passed forgotten grace.

205 Remembering

We go places, linger a bit,
meeting people on the way
to leave them.
Never we go back to those places.
I met you once
but do you remember?
How many people did I forget,
they walked in and out of my life.
I loved some of them deeply.
Some of them were my lovers
but they walked on
like I go to new places.

206 Forgotten Love

By now I'm sure you have forgotten me,
I on my part, try hard to do the same,
but in silent moments I say your name
and think about our lives, how it should be.

I felt well, while being closer to you,
this nearness showered me with joy and hope,
and gave me courage to go on and cope,
much more than just those silly phone calls do.

But now you have moved on, away from me.
Your phone is dead, the mailman has no mail,
and my autonomy will soon prevail,
back being one, alone, as I shall be.

We were just pedestrians on our way,
both not meant to stop, not meant to stay.

207 Marks of What Has Been

All got a new order from the day you left.
You even took your ragged up coat and
I rearranged the furniture.
Where your chair had stood for years
was a light mark on the wooden floor
that I tried to cover with a too small rug.
It came all the way from Mecca,
and had a nice shade of green.

I removed your photos one by one,
those that were too dear to look at,
out of the album where white spots remained,
the paper's original colour.
I took off your ring, the bracelet you gave me,
the necklace with the medallion, too,
and my skin was whiter
where the silver had been.

I thought removing your traces
would make me forget and
make me feel less sad,
but every white spot is you.
Your absence is leaving marks
reminding me of days of innocence,
where around them time has moved on,
unheard, unknown, unseen.

208 Coloured Memories of You

Most memories of you by now are painted
in shades of sunrises and oranges.
The dark has faded into sepia
and if I wait some more, you'll be all white.

Most facts of what went on, are futile dots,
unnoticed on the canvas near your face.
I've known you in all colours of this life
but I would tear the painting if it showed.

Most dreams of you are better than the truth.
Each time I find you back there under layers
of paint, and if I close my eyes, why would
I think of you but in sweetest colours.

209 So Much of What I Knew

You were so much of what I knew as life,
you went and never I had felt such pain,
no part of this great love remained with me.
I lived alone and loss had shown us how.

You went and never I had felt such pain,
when others said it had been for the best
I lived alone. And loss had shown us how
you found your rest. I cannot sleep at nights.

When others said it had been for the best
as they would never understand just how
you found your rest. I cannot sleep at nights,
I miss your hand, your eyes, your love.

As they would never understand just how
our bodies yearn for those they cannot see.
I miss your hand, your eyes, your love.
My nights are darker than a grave could be.

210 Recipe for a Memory

To remember you by,
I take a bit of sandalwood
smelling like the soap you used,
a drop of spring rain water,
a ray of sunshine dust
as the light fell
on our mornings,
and a tear, and blend it
in a night with silent
cobalt skies, to inhale
and drink your memory
just sip by sip
to feel that you
are with me, in me, near.

211 Airing the Orphanage

You had gone, leaving stuff:
a sock, two cotton handkerchiefs,
a CD with a cracked cover, a giant coffee mug,
and me. Dust was collecting on all of us.
Numb we stared at each other.
Waiting. One day you would need your mug.

Now it is spring. I opened the window
and fresh air is entering the orphanage.
I caress the crack on the CD cover,
and throw it away with the sock
and the handkerchiefs.
I keep the mug. And myself,
if you don't mind. To remember you
and whom you never were.

212 You Are So Not There

I feel familiar lines
on a shell I found
where the tide line ends.
It looks just like the shell
that you once gave to me.

I feel your skin touching my own.
I hear a voice in roaring sea
as it greets me every time,
and I hear you speak to me
in the same familiar tone.

The clouds are moving on so fast,
going east now in the shape
of your calmly waving hands,
the salt I'm tasting on my lips
is like the tears that you once shed.

All my senses seem aware
that you are with me now at last
but the beach is cold and empty,
the angry sea is without ships,
and you my friend are so not there.

213 The Coldest Cold

Many apparitions of cold don't bother me:
I don't care for the cool of the glass
against my feverish head
nor the breeze in summer
that makes the night bearable
but the windows clap,

nor the frost in your eyes
that won't look me in the face
as I ignore the icicles from your breath
when you feel the need to speak at last;
I have learned to dress warm.

Never though I'd get used
to the dog's indifference,
now you are his boss
and I a pedestrian walking by.

214 I've Sensed You for a While

I've sensed you for a while
in ordinary features of the morning
like Lipton tea and my warm winter coat.
In memories you were,
coming from the scent of cinnamon.
I've sensed you, on my body, in my skin.
You lingered in my mind.
Shivering under your illusive touch,
I felt your breathing through my hair.
In cold draft vales from open doors
I sensed your presence.
You warmed my sight in autumn colours.
In darkness, inside of me at night,
I sensed that we were one.
I heard your name in every sentence.
Still, for you, I was not even close in thought,
while you were living in my every breath.
Lately I've sensed you; for a while
you made me glad I was your lover
beyond all sense and your senseless death.

215 After You

I think a while you were the ghost
who lived with me and my two cats,
the grey one scared of you the most
and one indifferent to the world.

The room you'd painted blue before
had been a place for both of us,
'twas where we found our ways and more
through paths inside the other's mind.

And here it was where we made love
as if our love was still alive,
as if you could still find enough
in sharing it with cats and me.

I aired the room, your ghost won't leave
but lingers in the curtain's folds
reminding me how hard I grieve,
and what's the use, as time goes on.

216 Finding Peace Now

Night dragging on through hours
and you didn't show.
Mornings missed in days
I stood near the high waves
and you didn't show,
not even when the sea calmed down.
You stayed out of memories,
nights, days, and again nights,
but only after hearing of your death
I really slept.

217 You Are Not Dead

every life is you
in birds you sing for me
in flowers I can sense your scent
I see you in travelling clouds
that never reach the earth
and in every other child
there's you
every tear is mine
in rain they fall for me
in morning dew they glisten
and you appear in every drop
that hesitates to fall
and in every other love
there's you

218 Cold Rain

There are days of constant rain
like when we listened both,
and there will be more of those,
I shall listen on my own,
the sound of it, the countless drops,
a persistent background river.

There are days of constant dripping,
reminding me of our silence,
those will be there,
more days of constant pain,
the memory of constant rain,
the sound of it. The shiver.

And every drop carries your name,
each one a bullet sent to hurt.
Those are days of endless gunshots
till the last ones tick away.
Cold the air then, back to silence,
still remaining guilt and quiver.

219 Exactly Where You Are Not

I have not been there lately
as you still linger, sitting by that tree,
you are in sunlight, though it is a misty morning
or a grey autumn afternoon,
even in snow you are there
and I know I just want to touch you
so I haven't been there lately
and to be exact, neither have you.

220 Away From It All

Moving away from all things impossible
into better fields with buttercups and daisies
in evening sunshine with friends near the sea,
you will notice it was always waiting there.

And there will be memories in future
of laughter and salty moist at night;
all is already there, so you will find it
after moving away from impossible things.

221 Button

The day after you died,
the house still in awe,
a button fell off
of your best jacket
that hung, forlorn,
as if waiting for you,
over a kitchen chair
like you could enter
the door any minute.

The sound the button made
was too loud for its size
or importance as item,
when it slowly rolled,
halfway across the floor,
then making a turn
before it disappeared
under the skirting,
never to be seen again.

222 Bird Screams

I've waited longer than a mind can take,
a body can endure. Be independent is
what I am taught, and I am not. I needed
so to know someone can love me like I felt for you.

So often we mistake a bird for our soul.
We don't have wings, for starters,
we are lame. We need to name each other
and we wait, till the mind can take no more.

The sea was patient for my thoughts,
she always whispered good advice
until a bird flew over me and screamed
that I am lame for searching on the shore.

I've waited longer than I could endure or take,
and every bird became a cruel reminder.
Yet, with each wave that brought a shell, I knew
you had been mine, before you let me go.

I took a shell home every day in all those years
that you are gone. My tears have dried by now.
The birds became my friends. I know their cries
are not of you or me. They think we have no soul.

223 Messages

You sent me messages after your death
in paper headlines (Yes! He Will Be Back!)
and German number plates containing words
the meaning only you and I would know.

Maybe I should have let your presence go;
it's true that thinking of you always hurts,
but I can feel your eyes still in my neck
as I do sense the sound of your cold breath.

224 Your Mac

Between a winter jack and a nylon furry coat
your Mac is hanging there, as if you might return,
as if you aren't dead at all. Your scent is still afloat
between a winter jack and a nylon furry coat,
your boots—with all the dirt still from the road
attached, not cleaned—are nobody's concern.
Your Mac is hanging there, as if you might return,
as if you aren't dead at all. Your scent is still afloat.

225 Reconstruction

I reconstruct you bit by bit
from memory and from desire.
All of you comes back to me:
the way your arm would hold our son
and the spot there in your neck
where I can see that part of you
that you can't see yourself.
I build you up from wasted parts
like moments thrown away
and pieces of our broken hearts,
I make you mine again,
but this time tall and slender.
Bit by bit you reappear to me
in reconstructed tender.

226 Looking for Comfort on an Empty Beach

No message came to comfort me this time.
It was not hiding in some poem's rhyme,
in the sand was only sand to find.
A barren feeling of the cruellest kind
came over me, to know: we are alone
where all is true, when we are on our own,
a beach is just the end of land, no more.
I can not find my answer on this shore.

227 Back to Earth

Since the funeral a lot has changed.
From the moment we planted your body
into the sandy soil of your birth ground
trees started to grow faster and bigger.
Flowers produced more scent,
and see how the grass is no longer grass
but your hair, waving in wind. Gently. Kind.
A lot has changed. I love you now.

About the Author

Ina Schroders-Zeeders was born in the Netherlands, on the beautiful tourist-destination island of Terschelling. Her fascination with the sea began at an early age as she and her mother would frequently accompany her Merchant-Marine-Captain father on his adventures. Ina has spent her whole life enjoying books of all kinds, staying involved with libraries and book sales, until finally becoming a novelist in the late nineties. She remains on Terschelling with her husband.

www.ingramcontent.com/pod-product-compliance
Lightning Source LLC
Chambersburg PA
CBHW060011050426
42448CB00012B/2694